To Ann —
Best wishes —
Edwy Love

Ida,
the Gift-Wrapping Clydesdale

Ida,
the Gift-Wrapping Clydesdale

A Book of Humorous Verse

by

Edward Lodi

Rock Village Publishing
Middleborough, Massachusetts
―――――――
First Printing

Dedication

This book is dedicated to all the non-gift-wrapping but otherwise gainfully employed Clydesdales at Eastover Farm in Rochester, Massachusetts.

Acknowledgments

A number of the poems in this collection have previously tickled the funny bone (or irritated the spleen) as follows:

in *Beyond . . .* : "Maxims;"

in *Bifrost*: "Dracula;"

in *Cranberry Chronicles*: "Ode to the Rodent Clan," "The Virgin Earth;"

in *Ellery Queen's Mystery Magazine*: "Psycho" (in a slightly different version from the one included here);

in *Figment*: "King Kong;"

in *Light: A Quarterly of Light Verse*: "Cleri / hew," "Down to Earth," "Fice," "Ida, the Gift-Wrapping Clydesdale," "Ode to the Rodent Clan," "Road Rage," "Ubi Sunt?," "What Every Gardener Knows," "Why the Mantis Prays," "The Wolverine;"

in *Mediphors*: "Respiratory Blues;"

in *The Middleboro Gazette*: "The Winter of '96."

Contents

Bodily Health

Felons and Fiends

Invocation

From gaucheries and verbosities
and long-winded redundancies
and gaffes that give bumps to our prose
good grammar deliver us!

Friends: Finned, Feathered, and Furred

IDA, THE GIFT-WRAPPING CLYDESDALE

Ida, the gift-wrapping Clydesdale,
greets folks with a swish of her tail
and alluding to her allergy to hay
says, with a toss of her head and a neigh:

"Since it beHOOVES me to please,
I'll try not to sneeze
as I wrap your boxes with crepe
and fanciful paper and colorful tape.

"Please help me with one little thing;
put your finger on this loose string
and assist me in tying this knot.
(My iron-shod feet are clumsy, God wot!)"

The Wolverine

Of all earth's fearsome creatures
who lack redeeming features
the most mean
is the wolverine.

It makes a mess
of the wilderness.

Seeking a midnight snack
it'll raid a hunter's shack
and tear it to pieces,
leaving only the stench of feces,
or musk, or urine
(for which there's no curin').

Its species name is *gulo gulo*.
But don't let that fool you.
In Latin it's "glutton," double.
A wolverine means trouble!

Though its favorite food is carrion
it will eat anything you're carryin'.

A wolverine will scare
even a ferocious bear
and doesn't mind
eating porcupine.

It lacks decorum.
It takes only one to make a quorum.

It likes cold places like the tundra.
No wondra
even cougars eschew it.
If you ever meet one, you'll rue it.

I'd Rather Be a Bear

I'd rather be
a bear
than be
a bee.

I couldn't bear
to be
a bee.

I'd rather hector
trout
than scout
for nectar.

I'd rather prowl
and growl
the day away
than buzz
the way
a fuzz-
y
bee does.

It's not my thing
in spring
to tilt a wing
and sting.

I'd rather be a bear
with hair
and roar
like a carnivore,
and use my jaw
or paw
or claw.

What—me thrive
in a populous hive?
Pure jive!

If given a choice
and an ursine voice
I'd crave
a cave
or a hollow tree
just for me

and a she
bear
with whom to share
my lair—

a grizzly her
with frizzly fur
who seeks a mate
to share her fate
and hibernate.

A bee,
in sum,
is not much fun,
a sexless drudge
whom I'd begrudge
if he
(or she?)
were
me.

ODE TO THE RODENT CLAN

A vole
or a mole
is tiny and neat,
a pleasure to meet
as you walk in the woods
amid nature's goods.

A squirrel
whose fur will
fluff in the breeze
will surely please.

A hare
has a definite flair,
and even rabbits
have winsome habits,
ears that flop
as they frolic and hop.

A possum's
a rodent too, I think
though quite unlike a mink.
An unfortunate trait
is its awkward gait.
If I may speak plainly.
a possum's ungainly.

There's nothing awesome
about a possum.

Don't Be an Ass!

mule: the offspring of
a male ass and a female horse

hinny: the offspring of
a female ass and a male horse

If you hear a whinny,
and think it made by a mule,
don't be a fool, you hear?
Don't be a ninny!
It could be a mule you hear.
Or it could be a hinny.

Ubi Sunt?

(Where Are They Now, the Birds of Yesteryear?)

The Great Auk (cousin to the guillemot)
once was, but now is not.

Of the Passenger Pigeon
there remains not a smidgen.

The Woodpecker, Ivory-billed?
Long ago killed!

Likewise the Dodo
(whose intellect was so-so)
shares this sad distinction:
hunted to extinction.

When will these wrongs be righted?
When humans are similarly plighted!

FICE

variant of feist:
a small dog of mixed ancestry
(from obsolete "fist," to break wind)

Most agree a pedigree
is nice. Precise.
You get a pet
of high degree
and charge a fee,
big checks,
for sex,
win cups for pups.

Not me.

I prefer a cur
of ancestry
with mystery,
a fice
whose price
is free,
a mutt a cut
above the norm
whose form
though lacking symmetry
suits me.

The Cormorant

The cormorant
is ignorant
of etiquette.

Of fish
(its favorite dish)
it eats all it can get.

Its contents abdominal
are abominable.

With an urge
to purge
it doesn't hesitate
to defecate
but lets loose
like a sluice.

Its manure
has no allure.

Methinks
it stinks.

THE POLECAT

On the zoological chart
the polecat
is neither part,
nor whole, cat.

It does not purr.
"Cat" is merely a *nom de guerre*.
Nor, on any occasion,
is it ever of Polish persuasion.

Stink, stank, stunk
best conjugates this punk.
To be precise:
on the scale of nice
this "cat" would flunk.
I mean, of course, the skunk.

HOME INVASION

A scourge
hard to purge—
a curse
far worse
than a mouse
or rat—
is a bat
in your house.

Though no gent,
nor heaven-sent,
a flightless rodent
has in its favor
this behavior:
it *doesn't* fly
or *even* try
to go up high.

You can't say that
about a bat.

A bat spreads dread
above your head
and will defile
your domicile.

A bat is not
easily caught.

Please!
Forget about cheese.
It won't happen:
you simply can't trap him

(or her;
not every bat's a sir).

No cat—
no feline,
no ball of fluff—
can make a beeline
fast enough
to catch a bat.

So how do you nab it?
Jump
and give it a thump?
Absurd!

Grab it
as you might a rabbit?
My word!

A bat's too quick
to give it a lick
with a heavy stick.

Drat it,
there's no way
to bat it,
that is to say,
*un*bat it.

The Cassowary

(The Doublewattled Cassowary, native to New Guinea and Australia, attains a weight of up to 130 pounds and a height of six feet. This member of the ratites—a group of flightless birds—is known for its ill temper and is considered the only bird dangerous to humans.)

You need not fear,
you may assume,
the Rhea,
a flightless bird
of whom
no doubt you've heard.

An Ostrich
though you cross it
will never hold you hostich.

An Emu,
too
—you may intuit—
will be nice to you
if you're nice to it.

But alas! Be wary
of the Cassowary,
a fowl
known to disembowel
if confronted
or affronted.
Its sharp claw
knows no law
except that of "Nuts to you!"
and will rip the guts from you.

DECEPTIVE LABELING

The *cowbird*,
it should come as no shock,
flies not in a *herd*
but a flock.

THE COWBIRD

The cowbird
is a strictly "here and now" bird.

On the plains
it once took pains
to follow the buffalo
(*bison* to those in the know)
but for a long time now
has mostly followed the cow
eating bugs and other treats
kicked up by the cows' feets.

This "songbird" with a head of bronze
has a voice that's harsh—unlike Sarah
Vaughan's!

It's a parasitic pest,
laying eggs in other species' nests.
Its chick then steals the food
from its foster parents' brood.
Worse, the greedy lout
often pushes the others out.

This opportunistic bird
is best neither seen nor heard!

E Pluribus You Numb?

If two,
it's *you*,
not *yous*

but two *ewe*
are *ewes*

and *yew* and *yew*
are *yews*.

Does this confuse?
If so, use
you, not *yous*

but choose
(you can't lose)
cari*bou*
or cari*bous*.

THE TURKEY VULTURE

Concerning culinary culture
the turkey vulture
is less than fastidious—
It's downright hideous.

Its preferred cuisine
is grossly obscene.

Referring to its diet,
some might say, "Try it!"
But most would say, "Nay,"
to foods that decay.

By way of synopsis:
it eats rotting corpses.

THE FISH CROW

As every school child knows
fish are never crows
nor—no matter how one wishes—
are crows ever fishes.

Does the Fish Crow, then, exist?
Yes. On every birder's list.

No chimera is he, of feathered fin,
no mythical beast that can both fly and swim,
no legend of which you've never heard.
The Fish Crow's a real, live, flesh-and-blood bird.

The fish crow (shall we call him F.C.?)
spends most of his time by the sea
where he frolics
eating carrion fish and smashed mollusks.

F.C.'s smaller than his bro.
(the common, AKA American, crow).
And there's nothing else about him you need know.

THE BLUE JAY

(Blue Jays make a variety of sounds, some harsh, others musical, and can do a remarkable imitation of a Red-shouldered Hawk.— Peterson Multimedia Guides™: North American Birds)

The Blue Jay
has its say
in a most vociferous way.

It will quote
with a jarring note
(or mock
with a squawk)
a bird of prey.

One gimmick
is to mimic
the red-shouldered hawk
precisely.

A jay prefers screeches
to quiet speeches,
but if given feed'll
queedle
nicely.

Things Crawly and Creepy

Why the Mantis Prays

The male mantis when wed
approaches the conjugal bed
with anticipatory dread,
knowing his Mrs. may devour his head
—and on a whim
the rest of him—
without waiting
till they've finished mating.

A Ringneck Whose Neck I'd Like to Wring

(Ringneck—*Diadophis punctatus*—a small
snake with a yellow neck ring)

I found a golden ring—
like a wedding band—
in an earthen pot,
buried in the sand.

It was autumn.
I was cleaning out the pot.
The ring was at the bottom,
where a ring shouldn't ought.

All summer long
the terra cotta
had held pretty flowers
just like it oughta.

It stood by the shed
near the garden path.
Now the flowers were dead.
Time to give the pot a bath!

I emptied it of soil
and shook the pebbles out,
all according to Hoyle—
no need to rant and shout,

until I stuck my hand inside
and felt a creature squirm:
too small to be a turtle,
too big to be a worm!

All at once I dropped the pot.
Luckily it didn't break.
You'd have dropped it, too,
if you had grabbed a snake.

Slugfest

Though cousin to the snail
the slug is frail
and lacks a shell. He
walks upon his belly
and is thus a *gastropod*
or "belly foot."

Though unshod
he won't stay put.

Always on the go
the slug moves slow
(he never sprints)
and leaves no prints
save, from time to time,
a trail of slime.

Without even a "Beg your pardon"
this gluttonous herbivore
will chew upon your garden
till there's simply no more.

But be of good cheer:
like many a clod
this gastropod
is fond of beer.

All you need do
is fill a deep dish
with leftover brew
and watch the fool perish
(see the clown
drown)
by getting drunk
and going *ker-plunk*!

Midsummer Nightmare

This balmy night
in June
don't swoon
with fright.

Don't crouch
behind the couch
in positions fetal.

That weird rasping
that's got you gasping
all in a heap,

that incessant scratch
at your window screen
and storm door latch

that makes you leap
from bed
and scream
with dread

is no thug
breaking in
to commit a sin.

It's just a bug—
a harmless beetle.

The Inchworm

(also called Measuring Worm, Spanworm, Looper)

The inch-
worm
will in a pinch
squirm
horridly
in order to move forwardly.

Sometimes it falls.
Frequently it stalls,
getting no place
at a frantic pace.

Resolutely it hoops
itself into loops
and progresses
like Siamese Messrs.

Its trick
is to kick
with a bodily flick,
forming a hump
with its head and its rump,

drawing its rear
up close to its ear—
repeat-
ing this feat
with debonair
flair
and hardly a blooper.

Hooray for the looper!

Rocky

Rocky, the prize-fighting python,
boxes without any gloves on.
      Lacking two fists
      he's a pugilist
who bites—like Mr. Tyson.

A Poem for Mother's Day

Spiderlings
are fragile things,
hardly
a bite
for the tiniest
mite,
spindly,
and quite
petite.

Why
then
does their
mom,
when
they hatch,
try
to catch
and eat
some?

The question begs:
lacking veneration
for the next generation,
why lay eggs?

THE STINK BUG

Is it ever correct,
politically,
to call an insect
(however uncritically)
a "stink" bug?

Is it apropos
to refer to b.o.?

After all, the stink bug
is I think *bug*
in the true sense:
that is (without pretense
and in all respect)
a fore-winged insect
(and here's the crux)
with a mouth that sucks.

If you grab it,
this bug has a habit
that's nasty, it's true; *id*
est, from glands 'neath its belly
it squirts a fluid
that's horrifically smelly.

But is it fair to heap shame
on this juice-sucking bug
with a beak for a mug
by including "stink" in its name?

Would it not make *you* blench
to be known solely for your stench?

OF MATTERS TERRESTRIAL

THE VIRGIN EARTH

Imagine how the earth was when unmarred—
   with nothing tarred,

Oceans clean and pure, and air with no pollutants—
   and no genetic mutants.

Conjure up a scene of clear days followed by dark nights—
   no artificial lights.

Picture if you can no urban sprawl—
   no streets at all,

And dream of a world with species ranging free—
   with no you or me.

DOWN TO EARTH

In autumn
the merest
breeze
stirs
the trees
and pocks
the air
with sloughed off
leaves.

I like
the ease
with which
these
float,
then
with a jolt
touch
bottom.

What Every Gardener Knows

Among my gardening woes
(besides a stuffed-up nose)
I number: blistered toes,
a blight-afflicted rose,
a host of insect foes,
a leaking plastic hose
with nozzle that won't close,
seeds an ill wind blows,
thieving flocks of crows,
marauding bucks and does,
and neatly tended rows
where *nothing* ever grows.

WHEN THE EARTH QUAKES . . .

Ironic,
isn't it,
that plates tectonic
don't quite fit.

Is it God's intent
that the continents
be incontinent?

THE BLIZZARD OF '78

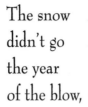

The snow
didn't go
the year
of the blow,

the year
the nor'easter
knocked us
on our keister.

It lasted until
Easter.

THE WINTER OF '96

Last week it snowed
a blizzard—rough;

last night again,
a powdery fluff

and in between
more of the stuff.

It's pretty, sure,
but enough's enough!

MAXIMS

Maxim (I)

Don't go near a hole in space.
You wouldn't like the hectic pace.
You'd find it hard to keep your place.

If a hole in space you find,
It's not a figment of your mind,
Just a lack (of every kind).

Maxim (II)

If the speed of light you go,
Year by year you younger grow.
At least, your friends all think you so.

When you go the speed of light
Expect your day to turn to night.
Or night to day; each way is right.

MAXIM (III)

If a comet should come nigh
You'll see it in the evening sky.
Don't breathe the air as it goes by.

Impress upon your mind this fact:
A comet can, without impact,
Afflict a world with ruin and wrack.

Pertaining to the Gastric

On the Chew Chew

Clack
  clack
    clack
along the track

All decked out
  you strain
to shout
  above the din

and lurch about
  and slop din din
upon your chin

  and spill champagne—
on the Dinner Train.

A Wino No More

When I was a loser
I was just a boozer.

But now that I drink in style
I'm an oenophile!

The Dyspeptic Diplomat

He has no wish
for a spicy noodle dish,

but he lives in Thailand
and will try and

be glad
to serve pad thai

in his Thai pad.

The Mangelwurzel

(a variety of beet with a large yellow root, used chiefly as food for cattle)

Its skin is rough,
its flesh is yellow.
It's always tough,
never mellow.

A
mangelwurzel
is a beet—
no doubt the
worst you'll
ever eat.

BODILY HEALTH

Respiratory Blues

Of all the petty ills that blight us
(their intent, it seems, to spite us)
I dislike the most bronchitis.

It's pneumonia's little tease—
lets you breathe, but with a wheeze.
You cough, and then you sneeze.

Of all the germs that tire us
and in a cold sweat mire us
I hate that bronchial virus.

Diagnosis

If you pout
and shout
and hobble about,
there's no doubt
you lout—
you've got the gout!

Felons and Fiends

Be Meek. Inherit.

Is your uncle wealthy,
and not very healthy?
Be stealthy!

Avoid a glitch.
Get rich
without a hitch.

Don't annoy
the old boy
with an obvious ploy.

Don't request
a bequest
at his behest.

Try
to be sly.
Lie.

Inveigle.
Finagle.
Then poison his bagel.

To a Failed Assassin

(It's so confusin',
sticking that fuse in.)

Though you were bent
with murderous intent,
you lacked aplomb
constructing your bomb.

It's here, in the obits—
you blew yourself to bits.

Cleri-
hew

(clerihew: a humorous poem about a person who is usually named in the first line)

Al Ca-
pone
called it
home

whereas
I call it
Al Ca-
traz

Psycho

His loves were mixed up with his hates.
He did strange things to his dates.
He liked to put on
The guise of his Mom—
A regular cut-up, that Bates.

Dracula

The count! So ancient, yet crude.
Undead, but hopelessly lewd.
    A creature most sanguine
    When sinking his fang in
A lady both buxom and nude.

Altered Ego

Dr. Jekyll to Mr. Hyde:
"What a hassle having *you* inside!
If we split in two
I'll be rid of you."
They did. He was. Then he died.

King Kong

An unfortunate ape named Kong
had ideas that were morally wrong.
He wanted his way
with actress Fay Wray
but his notion was simply too long.

Frankenstein's Monster

Embroidered with stitches and creases,
He's a wonder that never ceases:
A menace at large
This human collage
Comprised of bits and pieces.

Two Drunkards Discuss the Afterlife, and the Disposal of Their Remains

First Imbiber

"Beverage
gives me leverage.
Nothing can harm me.
There's no need to embalm me.
I've got fluid in my veins
and pickled brains.

When those mournful church bells toll
and I'm buried in a hole—
when my soul
and body sever—
my remains
will last forever."

Second Imbiber

"I, too,
I think,
am soused with drink.
Like you,
I'm tickled
to be pickled
while up here.

But when I'm dead
I want a head
that's clear.

I fear
with booze
I'm sated.

When I expire
I desire
—I choose—
to be cremated."

Envoi

About eternity
These two could not agree,
and upon their demise
they made no compromise.

One was stewed,
the other barbecued.

BYOB

(jeroboam: a wine bottle which holds four-fifths of a gallon and is therefore equal to two magnums. The term derives from the biblical Jeroboam, a mighty king who caused Israel to sin.)

When folks who drink hearty
arrive at your party
you'll know 'em
by their jeroboam
(defined in this poem).

An Ancient Curse, Wrought into Verse

If rats were chickens
I'd cook up a stew
with the main ingredient—
you guessed it!—*you.*

Road Rage

Do not go gentle
as you drive
along at night.
Whatever your direction,
at each intersection
rage,
rage against the changing
of the light.

Do it!
If the signal's red
go through it.

Go fast.
Step on
the gas.
Keep that rubber peeled.
Your car's a weapon
you need never yield.

If like Grandpa Grunt
the guy in front
drives slower than treacle,
bop his vehicle.

Even if the fellow
who makes you bellow
is your brother,
cuss out his mother.
Don't linger.
Throw the finger.

Be never wrong.
Be always right.
Get out of your car
and into a fight.

SMILE

IF YOU LIKE THIS FORTUNE COOKIE

*T*he following one-act play is presented to readers of Ida, the Gift-Wrapping Clydesdale as a lagniappe. Though not in verse, it was written in the same spirit as the poems in this collection.

All of the dialogue, as well as the title of the play—everything, in fact, except for the stage directions—represents exact transcripts of fortunes received by the author on slips of paper contained in fortune cookies at Chinese restaurants. He has not changed a word. (But he has consumed a lot of Chinese food.)

SMILE IF YOU LIKE THIS FORTUNE COOKIE

A Play in One Act

List of Characters
(in alphabetical order)

HE: a man

SHE: a woman

WAITER: a person (of either sex)

TIME: the present

PLACE: a Chinese restaurant

SETTING: a table for two. HE and SHE are seated so that they face one another and the audience. Although WAITER does not speak until the end, he or she is present on the stage throughout the play and engages in waiterly activities.

HE

(to the audience)   This is the month when ingenuity stands high on the list. There's a good chance of a romantic encounter soon. Now is the time to try something new.

(to SHE)   A quiet evening with a friend is the best tonic for a long day.

SHE

(to HE)   You're a bundle of energy, always on the go.

HE

(to SHE)   It's a good thing that life is not as serious as it seems to the waiter.

SHE

(to HE)   A sense of humor is a great asset.

HE

(to the audience)   Be direct. Usually one can accomplish more that way.

(to SHE)   You are in good hands this evening. A thrilling time is in your immediate future.

(to the audience)   Get your mind set—confidence will lead you on. Go after what you want. There's no time like the present. People always admire your patience and ability to persevere.

(*to SHE*)   Good things are being said about you.

SHE

(*to HE*)   You have a reputation for being straightforward and honest.
(*to the audience*)   Trust him, but keep your eyes open.
(*to HE*)   Your cheerful outlook is one of your assets. You're sociable and entertaining.

HE

(*to the audience*)   Sell your ideas. They are totally acceptable. Be sincere—even when you don't mean it!
(*to SHE*)   It's time to explore new interests. The night life is for you. You may attend a party where strange customs prevail. Give a kiss to the person who sits next to you.

SHE

(*to the audience*)   It is better to deal with problems before they arise.
(*to HE*)   You have an active mind and a keen imagination. Do not mistake temptation for opportunity.

HE

(*to the audience*)   Avert misunderstanding by calm,

poise, and balance. Every truly great accomplishment is at first impossible.

(to SHE)   You are a very bright individual. You're the center of every group's attention. Life to you is a dashing and bold adventure.

SHE

(to the audience)   Keep your feet on the ground even though friends flatter you. A liar is not to be believed even though he tells the truth.

(to HE)   Love is like war: easy to begin but hard to stop.

HE

(to the audience)   Bide your time for success is near.

(to SHE)   The heart is wiser than the intellect. What's a vice today may be a virtue tomorrow. Be prepared to accept a wondrous opportunity in the days ahead!

SHE

(to the audience)   Answer just what your heart prompts you.

(to HE)   The pleasure of what we enjoy is lost by wanting more.

HE

(to the audience)   A pound of pluck is worth a ton of luck.

(*to SHE*)   You have a potential urge and the ability for accomplishment.

SHE

(*to the audience*)   One look is worth ten thousand words.

HE

(*to SHE*)   You're cautious in showing your true self to others. You have a curious smile and a mysterious nature. Beauty surrounds you with every step you take.

(*to the audience*)   Money speaks a language everyone understands.

(*to SHE*)   You will receive many beauteous gifts in the years ahead.

SHE

(*to the audience*)   You are heading in the right direction.

(*to HE*)   All the world may not love a lover but they will be watching him.

HE

(*to the audience*)   Diligence is the mother of good fortune. All your hard work will soon pay off! Your dearest wish will come true.

(*to SHE*)   You are in for an enlightening experience.

SHE

(*to HE*) A modest man never talks of himself.

HE

(*to SHE*) Your heart will always make itself known through your words.

SHE

(*to the audience*) Enjoy life! It is better to be happy than wise.

(*to HE*) You will always get what you want through your charm and personality. The world is always ready to receive talent with open arms.

HE

(*to the audience*) Pardon is the choicest flower of victory. Good to begin well. Better to end well.

(*to SHE*) Your winsome smile will be your sure protection.

SHE

(*to HE*) Some important decisions have already been made. Fortune is smiling on you!

HE

(*to the audience*) Extra effort has been necessary but it will pay off.

(*to SHE*) The old way has come to an end. Don't expect the ordinary.

WAITER

(*to HE and SHE*)   You may be hungry soon. Order a takeout now.

The End

AFTERWORD

Afterword

A question frequently asked of writers—by naive albeit well-wishing readers—is: "Where do you get your ideas?"

The answer of course is: "Over the Internet. Writers used to get their ideas from a toll-free number (1-800-GET-IDEA). But now we obtain them from a website (www.ideasforwriters.com)."

The price for ideas? A dime a dozen.

Actually, the idea for the poem, "Ida, the Gift-Wrapping Clydesdale," came to me one night in a dream. Just the idea. Not the words. Those I had to work for. The words I had to pluck from thin air and shape into a poem, line by line. But the title—and the concept of a horse who earns her living by wrapping gifts—came to me in a dream.

"Fice," on the other hand, was inspired by an actual dog—a black bantam mongrel I spotted while driving around Middletown, Rhode Island, one day with friends. (The dog wasn't driving, my friends and I were. But say— a fice driving around in a car and taking in the scenery might make for an amusing poem. I'll have to think about that one.)

The fice that I saw that day—sniffing its way and lifting its leg along the side of the road—was a classic example of the (non)species, i.e., it was unique (no two fices are *ever* alike); intelligent (fices have to be, to survive in a world of much larger dogs, not to mention mongrel-munching coyotes); asymmetric (most fices are lopsided); and pugnacious (the true fice is fearless and will stand up to an adversary many times its size). And—like all true fices—it exuded an aura (in equal proportions) of canine *sang-froid* and *savoir-faire*.

Members of the Animal Kingdom—be they spiders, insects, mammals, birds, reptiles, amphibians, or whatever—provide an endless source of inspiration for humorous verse. For example, I find the Fish Crow fascinating simply because of its name. How can a fish be a crow, or vice versa?

Whereas, with the Praying Mantis it's not the creature's name so much as its cannibalistic behavior when engaged in amorous activities that prompted a poem.

For many years I've known (though not from firsthand experience) of the hazards the male mantis faces when mating. However, it was in fact *after* the poem was published (in *LIGHT: The Quarterly of Light Verse*) that I came across the following in *Audubon* magazine: "Mantises are among the few insects that can swivel their heads. This talent allows a female to respond to an amorous male, stealthily approaching her from behind, by literally biting his head off, an admonishment that impairs his sexual performance not a whit." A recent issue of *Harper's* devoted a full page to a sequence of six photographs showing the male mantis approaching the female, etc. The mantis, it seems, has gained universal notoriety.

Notoriety of another sort—that of the fictional character Norman Bates (played by Anthony Perkins in the Alfred Hitchcock film version of Robert Block's novel)—inspired the limerick, "Psycho." Incidentally, this was one of the very first of my humorous verses to be published—in *Ellery Queen's Mystery Magazine*. For some bizarre reason, known only to the editors (and perhaps to the Norman Bateses of the world), someone at the magazine changed my five-line limerick to a four-line poem, an alteration which—in my humble estimation—much weakened it.

Who can plumb the depths of the psychotic—or editorial—mind?

An idea for a poem may come about through direct observation of the natural world. "The Blue Jay" is such a poem. I am fortunate to live in an area frequented by a variety of species of birds, including blue jays and red-shouldered hawks. The latter are notably vociferous when flying overhead; they make their presence readily and universally known.

Blue jays produce many sounds—including an almost perfect imitation of the red-shouldered hawk. Hence, the poem celebrating the mimicking abilities of the former. (*Queedle* is a more melodious song of the jay.)

I am also fortunate to live not too far from the Cape Cod Canal. The paved service roads on either side of the canal are a pleasant place on which to walk and watch the boat traffic, or observe the many species of birds, pelagic or otherwise, which visit the area. One such bird is the Double-crested Cormorant.

Cormorants will on occasion—along with gulls—perch atop the lamp posts that have been placed alongside the canal. And like the gulls, cormorants will on occasion relieve themselves. The sounds they produce when doing so I leave to the imagination of the reader. As for the odor, and the consistency of the resultant guano . . . my advice is, tread carefully and wear a broad hat when passing beneath a cormorant.

"A Ringneck Whose Neck I'd Like to Wring" accurately describes the incident that inspired it. While emptying out flower pots in the fall I stuck my hand into a large terra cotta pot to remove the pebbles from the bottom—and grabbed a snake (which, judging by its reaction, was even more startled than I).

The snake was a ringneck—harmless and like most snakes beneficial to the gardener. It had taken up residence at the bottom of the pot, presumably with the intention of spending the winter there. After I gave it the bum's rush it evidently found a suitable domicile elsewhere, for I spied it the following summer—unmistakable with its yellow neck ring and bright red belly—slithering under the shed.

It seems that I was fortunate in my encounter in

receiving only a momentary start. Research—in *National Audubon Society Field Guide to North American Reptiles and Amphibians*—reveals that the ringneck "Rarely attempts to bite when picked up, but will void musk and foul-smelling contents of the cloaca."

Is it, I wonder, soul-mate to the cormorant?

In addition to the quatrains in celebration of the contretemps with the ringneck, my passion for gardening has inspired many ideas for poems. "What Every Gardener Knows," for example, merely recounts—in rhyme—precisely what every gardener knows, i.e., that frustration abounds.

Likewise "Slugfest" describes—accurately, I hope—the many habits of the slug. And believe me—sardine cans or other suitable containers filled with beer do, effectively, trap the gluttonous creatures.

Speaking of slugs: on a recent trip to Maine my wife and I stayed at an inn located in a rural area. One evening, shortly before dusk, we went for a walk up the paved road that curves by the inn, and were appalled by the hundreds of dead slugs—road kill—that we encountered. In fact, in places the slimy remains of their bloated bodies made walking on the pavement hazardous. A local nature trail through the woods was likewise infested—though this time with live slugs. *Thousands.* So that with each step, it seemed, we trod upon ten or twelve. Surely there's matter here for humorous verse. Or a horror story, depending on one's mood or inclination.

A real-life horror story, the rampant extinction of numerous species brought about by human activities, inspired "Ubi Sunt."

The title derives from Latin: *"Ubi sunt qui ante nos fuerunt?"* "Where are those who lived before us?" The shortened phrase, *Ubi sunt*, refers to the time-honored convention or motif in literature—common throughout the ages, and especially in medieval times—the lament which emphasizes the transitory nature of life. The most famous example is probably François Villon's *"Mais où sont les neiges d'antan?"* "Where are they now, the snows of yesteryear?"

(Since writing the poem I have learned, from various sources, that there is a slight—an *extremely* slight—chance that the Ivory-billed Woodpecker may not be extinct after all. One ornithologist claims to have sighted a pair, and others claim to have heard the bird's distinctive call, in deep, remote woods. One hopes that these reports are true.)

A related poem, "The Virgin Earth," originated from wistful—or should that be *wishful*?—thinking: What if there were no people on the earth, and the world was allowed to be forever pure and unspoiled, "with species ranging free—

/ with no you or me?"

Of course, with no me, this book would not exist. And with no you, it would have no readers. But then—would that be so terrible a thing?

That last question is perhaps best left unanswered.

On the subject of terrible things: The "Invocation" with which I began this little volume is a takeoff on an ancient Scottish Invocation, to wit:

From ghoulies and ghosties
and long-legged beasties
and things that go bump in the night,
Good Lord deliver us!

And "Road Rage" derives its opening lines from a distortion of Dylan Thomas's poignant lines, "Do not go gentle into that good night / Rage, rage against the dying of the light." For which travesty, I ask of his spirit forgiveness.

In rather the same category as "A Ringneck Whose Neck I'd Like to Wring" is "Home Invasion," in that it was a product of home schooling, i.e., the School of Hard Knocks.

For three or four years after moving into our log house, my wife and I were plagued by an infestation of bats. (It only *seemed* like an infestation; actually the bats were infrequent visitors. But having a bat fall from the rafters onto your head while you're sound asleep at three o'clock in the morning qualifies, while it's happening, as a full-fledged invasion.) On more occasions than I care to remember I had to evict the pesky critters, either by opening windows and removing screens, in the hope that they would find their own means of egress, or by catching them in daylight (no easy matter in a log house with a loft) and forcibly evicting them.

Eventually, we found the tiny crack near the chimney through which the bats were entering the house, had it plugged, and have been bat-free ever since. But those first three or four years were interesting (in the ancient-Chinese-curse sense of the word—*may you live in interesting times*), a fact to which "Home Invasion" readily attests.

As for how my fevered brain came up with the idea for "Cleri / hew," all I can say is that I've always wanted to write one. A clerihew, that is. (It was either a clerihew or an epic—something à la *The Iliad* or *The Odyssey*—and clerihews are much shorter and somewhat easier to compose.) The form is named for Edmund Clerihew Bentley, who invented it. He wrote his first clerihew (about the famous scientist Sir Humphrey Davy) in school out of boredom while listening to a chemistry lecture.

The classic clerihew contains four lines, with a person's name in the first. You might want to try your hand at one. Here are two lines to start you off (you furnish the other two):

Edward Lodi

is hoity-toity

. . . .

. . . .

My editor tells me that I now have enough material to fill a book. So I'll end here.